Thank you for looking at

MORRIS PUBLISHING

Book Specifications

Binding: Perfect Binding
Cover: Cover Design Template #6.
  Ink: Turquoise and black
  Cover Stock: 10 pt.
  Texture: Marble
  Title Font: Baker Signet
  Copy Font: Berkeley
  Artwork: customer provided
Text: Camera-ready
# of Pages: 78 (including this page and 15 blank pages)
Text Paper: Heavier Paper -- 60 lb. white
Text Ink: Black
Special Pages: Title Page 1, Copyright Page, Title Page 2,
  Dedication Page, Table of Contents, Index of First Lines,
  and About the Author
Special Features: Illustrations

---

*Our commitment to excellence has made us
America's #1 short-run book printer. We are proud
to demonstrate the fine quality of our books.*

Out of Silence

From the Heart of the
San Jacinto Mountains

Selected Writings

Stephanie Chase

STONEHILL PRESS
IDYLLWILD • CALIFORNIA
1996

Grateful acknowledgment is given to the following publications in
which certain poems have appeared:
AMERICAN BARD, ARIZONA HIGHWAYS, BLUE MOON, DRIFTWIND,
FELLOWSHIP, FRIENDS JOURNAL, IDYLLWILD TOWN CRIER, PRAIRIE
WINGS, SUNDIAL AND VARIEGATIONS.

The material in this book was published previously by
Woodloft Limited Editions, as follows:
Of More Than Earth © 1965 by Stephanie Chase. ☆
Tall Magic © 1965 by Stephanie Chase. ☆
Imprint © 1972 by Stephanie Chase.
Leaf Song © 1989 by Stephanie Chase ⌐⌐⌐
Out Of Silence © 1993 by Stephanie Chase.
     ☆ The original edition was designed and printed with
          hand set type and hand cut blocks by Marvin Weese.
     ⌐⌐⌐ Illustrations by Val Samuelson.
Produced and designed from the original editions by
Idyllwild Typeset & Design
Book and cover design by Larry Morton
Illustration by Val Samuelson
Visit us on the web at www.pe.net/~itd

Published by
STONEHILL PRESS
P.O. BOX 493 IDYLLWILD, CA 92549

ISBN I-888834-005
Printed in the United States by:
Morris Publishing • 3212 East Highway 30 • Kearney, NE 68847

Out of Silence

From the Heart of the
San Jacinto Mountains

This book was made for Stefi,
without her knowledge (or consent!)
as a gift of gratitude and love.

She has touched so many,
so deeply,
through so many years.

Contents ✐

from

Of More Than Earth

Journey

Dark night –
and one star shining . . .
no heart so alien
to its way
that it cannot search
the darkness out –
and cross the shadows
into light . . .

Small Eternity

Nothing
is forever –
and yet –
love must have
its always . . .
even for a little while.

Postlude

My heart
is a snow-bird
upon a winter-bough –
singing your name
in white stillness.

Juncture

How can one explain
the sense of kinship
with another?
The swift togetherness
that does not wait
the slow design of words;
the warm content
that does not borrow
from desire.
This bright forging
of our days
is beyond the questioning –
it is enough to know
we have met again
to clasp this hour
of recognition.

Communion

The fullness
of one perfect hour
holding the timeless beat
of heart speaking to heart
spills over the waiting cup . . .
and I, the dreamer,
craving the draught –
sip each moment slowly . . .
slowly . . . to remember.

Of More Than Earth

No man can fall
whose quickened dreams have sped
the edge of time
to follow the starpaths
of the gods —
the measure of his song
will know its birth
in timelessness —
and be of more than earth.

from

Tall Magic

*H*ere,
the earth and sky
claim me
with a titan-hold.
City-born,
I remember thin, grey light
touching the cage-bottom
of my days – and no expanse
but the length and breadth
of hope.
And now – poised
between low and high –
I am not my own
but free . . .
a mountain lifts me
to the sky!

𝒯 he smallest foothill
lifts its way
to the mountain-peak.

The simplest faith
gains foothold
to the stars . . .

What proud spirit
marks this tree?
A forest god's enchanted aeon
turned to silent immortality –
or the soul of a woodland giant
spanning the reach
of an ageless dream?
Perhaps…a faithful seer
keeps vigil here –
guarding the wisdom
of the patient years.

Rain
is a roof
of bongo drums –
thunder-magic
in the night –
morning splashed
with diamond light.

The wind
stalks the night
like a restless
banshee – wailing
its loneliness
into the black
silence . . .

$\mathcal{M}$agic is the hearth
where the welcome-fire burns —
where joy lifts a beacon
in the gathering night —
and home is a step inside
the sheltering glow
of friendly hearts ...
where no man stands —
a stranger in the light.

*V*illage is a word
friendly as a hand-clasp,
warming as hearth-fire.
It is a gentle word
that speaks of simple things
and holds a quiet wonder.
A village belongs
to the forest,
to the mountains,
to those who follow
its magic pathways.
A village that is peopled
with love and goodness,
that knows each season's
blessings
is a world unto itself –
a peaceful world –
where the pilgrim heart,
done with its seeking,
stops to rest
in gratitude.

The earth is dressed
in white silence . . .
Snow-trees
swirl their mantles
to the ground . . .
from a crystal branch
a sparrow
sings his noel
to the sky!

$\mathcal{H}$ ere we have a timeless accent
on life . . . a chance to live
from the ground up –
to plant roots purposefully and,
like the trees, to point our growth
toward the stars.
Here – on every hand – we have the
measure of infinity around us.

$\mathcal{T}$ here is nothing stinting about
nature. Our blessings are easy to
count . . . open skies to pull our
vision upward – the strength of the
mountain bolstering our days . . .
above us and around us the visible
wonders of the Taller Strength.

$\mathcal{I}$ will take my prayer
to the mountains,
where the inviolate towers
shadow the silence
with holiness.
I will lift my words
out of the stillness —
and let them climb
the solitudes
beyond the stars.

from

Imprint

Urban Abstract

Cement blocks
of gray and glass
under a
falling-plaster sky —
blur of streets
and poles
and mud-wheel cars —
and people
vanishing through
to little gray jobs . . .
city phantoms.

Coffee Shop Collage

Counter square
of morning faces . . .
half masks,
whole masks,
mostly
one of a kind masks –
now and then
surprise masks,
exchanging
paper smiles
for the day.

Circles

Worlds colliding —
worlds exploding
angry worlds
pushing to the edge . . .
and in between
round-with-love worlds
making wider circles
against the madness.

Symbol

Leaning
against thin air,
I brace myself
with the memory
of a tree rooted in rock,
the growth
of its life
pushing out
from a crack of soil.

Rabbit
on the lawn,
still as the breath
I hold
watching you,
where are the fields
to hide you?
Cities
were not made
for the softness
of rabbits . . .

Trees
do not have
last words
before they die –
        only the stumps remain.
And those who mourn
with earth and sky
must carry the pain
for mute
and growing things
felled
in an instant.

She made patches
on patches
and we laughed
at her insistence
that even
the most frayed things
hold together.
Today I part with
things I cannot use,
all-of-a-piece,
good as new –
but the old, frayed things
she saved
are forever sewn
into my life
with double patches.

* to my mother

He loved weather-vanes
and was always
looking to see
if his was pointing
north or south . . .
it made a difference
to his days
to know which way
the wind was blowing . . .
and now the weather-vane
points north, south,
east, west —
and he watches
from where
the wind is born.

* to my father

from

Leaf Song

To M.W.
who loved the
autumn woods ...

To you
   heaven must be
eternal October,
where the trees
forever hold
   the flaming gold
    of autumn . . .
where the snows
of winter
   never fall
upon the stars . . .

October
shines the light
of a thousand suns
    through the trees . . .
the forest shimmers
    in golden stillness.

I am gold spun
in autumn,
orbiting with
the leaves –
whirled
in the wind . . .
my own ball
    of sun,
gathering light
    against the
        winter.

Paint your canvas bold!
Let the colors blaze
with sunset-fire
   and gold,
before these hours
   of autumn flame
      turn to a
         molten instant.

Someone
passing by?
Only the shuffle
of autumn leaves
in the wind.

To hold fast
or let go . . .
the autumn leaf
makes
no decision . . .

There is a pattern
    of quiet
in the golden light,
broken gently
by the shadow-fall
    of a drifting leaf . . .

Leaves
fall to earth
  one
  by
  one
into their own
togetherness.

from

Out of Silence

Walk the woods
with me . . .
walk gently here . . .
only the silence
will hold
the imprint
of our passing . . .

Full moon and saki —
suddenly, a falling star . . .
celestial haiku!

Shadows near the fence . . .
coyotes awaken my dogs
to howl at the moon.

Children on the road
leave a trail of laughter.
I follow their joy
as far as I can hear . . .

My dog's tail wagging . . .
more articulate than words
I speak in greeting.

Longer than haiku,
a dachshund
stretches his length
to a sonnet trot.

Rainy Day

The day
is wrapped
in a
mist-cocoon.
Soft grays fold me in . . .
my thoughts hold still,
like raindrops
on a leaf.

Snow falling . . .
white, pillowy silence
bedding the earth down
to quiet sleep . . .
soundlessly I fall
into the stillness
of myself –
like the snow
falling quiet . . .
falling deep . . .

Grey clouds hide the peaks.
When I look up tomorrow,
I will see the snow.

Earthquake

Wrenched
out of a nightmare,
the reality
of a split moment
gives a jagged twist
to life . . .
the night
is suddenly tilted,
shattered
and splintered.
The earthquake
makes mockery
of standing on solid ground.
Nothing is that firmly fixed.

Solace

The night
knows me
like no one
knows me.
It sees me
in my own light . . .
yielding to my own essence.
The hours
of the night do not nip
at my heels
like angry dogs
baiting me.
The night
is a friend
bringing me home
to myself
at the end of day.

The hawk sharpens
his talons
against
a lightning sky.

Men
with metal eyes
do not see
the stars . .

Flowers without scent,
like people without passion –
looking beautiful.

Quarry

One shot explodes
the autumn woods.
Heart pounding
in flight, I am the deer
running for life.

This could be
the year
without spring . . .
sun burning cold –
stars without light –
the days
caved under.
This could be
that time –
with the world
cut into pieces
of dying –
       in a year
          without spring.

Children
of the earth,
come out
of the darkness –
light your candles
from the stars . . .
Keep vigil
for all the world.
Let no heart
deny the other . . .
let your love
be the sign of peace
made visible.

Index of First Lines

Titles are in *italic*.

About the author

To Stephanie Chase, living in the woodland village of Idyllwild, in the heart of the San Jacinto Mountains, is poetry in itself.

Though her poems have appeared in various publications during many years of writing, she prefers to come out in print with small books of poetry. Stefi, as she is known to her friends, draws her inspiration from the mountains that surround her, giving her a perspective on life "from the top."

In the quiet of the forest she continues to write, aware of the fullness of life around her ... letting her poems "write themselves" in tribute to the mountain world that nurtures her spirit.